T'ain't Nobody's Business if I Do: Women Blues Singers Old and New

By Rhetta Akamatsu

Revised Edition

TABLE OF CONTENTS

Preface: Blues Women

The Way of the Blues

PART I: The Early Blues Women

PART II: Blues Women from the

60's to the Present

PREFACE: BLUES WOMEN

The early ones had to be tough. All of them were black. Some of them were big women, but even the small ones could hold their own in a fight.

They spent lots of time roughing it on the road, playing in juke joints and bars, or in tents in the middle of fields. They traveled in overcrowded, broken down trucks and cars, or on buses and trains. They ate at the backdoors of restaurants and in alleys, or at eating establishments for blacks only, and they slept in the homes of relatives or friends or in black boarding houses (many of which did not cater to entertainers.) Sometimes they slept in the cars or trucks.

When they made it big, like Ma Rainey or Bessie Smith, they bought their own private trains and many of them hung themselves about with jewelry and glitzy garments so they shimmered and shone when they shook as they sang. Then they were the "Queens":

"The queens, regal in their satins, laces, sequins and beads, and feather boas trailing from their bronze or peaches-and-cream shoulders, wore tiaras that sparkled in the lights. The queens held court in dusty little tents, in plush city cabarets, in crowded theaters, in dance halls, and wherever else their loyal subjects would flock to pay homage. They rode in fine limousines, in special railroad cars, and in whatever was available, to carry them from country to town to city and back, singing as they went. The queens filled the hearts and souls of their subjects with joy and laughter and renewed their spirits with the love and hope that came from a deep well of faith and will to endure." (1)

Making it or breaking, peasants or queens, they were the blues women, and they were there at the start of it all.

THE WAY OF THE BLUES

The early history of the blues is mainly an oral history. Generally, it is believed that the blues got their beginning in the Mississippi Delta following the Civil War, and evolved from the songs of field workers, dance tunes called "jump ups," church music, and traditional African music. It grew out of the "call and response" type of song, where a leader would call out a line and the guitar would answer.

The first form of blues was based on folk music. Some of the musicians performing this music played at carnivals and medicine shows, where they came in contact with country musicians, and vaudeville performers. Gradually, they evolved an entirely unique style, the blues as we know it. From Mississippi, the blues followed Highways 61 and 49 to Memphis, and also to New Orleans.

The first venues for black musicians were probably the minstrel shows, which became popular after the Civil War.

While they began with white performers in blackface, by the late 1800's, almost all the performers actually were black. The first black revue was probably "Jack's Creole Burlesque Show," owned by a white man named Jack Ingram, which opened in 1890. Blues greats Bessie Smith, Ma Rainey, and Ida Cox all started out in minstrel shows.

Medicine shows were probably the next venues for the black musicians. The so-called "doctors" who owned the shows traveled all around, looking for gullible customers to sell their herbal, and often mostly alcoholic, medications. Many rural areas lacked adequate medical care, and people were anxious for relief for their various aches and ailments. Black musicians were a cheap, easy draw to gather the crowd to hear the "doctor's" pitch.

The popularity of the medicine shows called out for a more permanent venue for the performers. In 1907, in Memphis, Tennessee, the first theatre for medicine show performers was opened by a man named Fred Barrasso. This theatre eventually led to TOBA, the Theatre Owners Booking Association, an organization that specialized in black music and black performers, and was responsible for the tours of many of the black female blues singers we are going to be discussing.

W.C. Handy was the first musician to popularize the blues in 1911-1912, but it was a woman, Mamie Smith, who really started the blues craze in 1920, when she recorded "Crazy Blues." We will look at Mamie Smith in more detail later.

Around this time, in the 1920's, many of the musicians on Beale Street in New Orleans left town, when Mayor "Boss" Crump shut down Beale to try to put an end to the drinking, gambling, prostitution, and general wild living taking place there. They headed for Chicago and Detroit, where the blues got electrified and became more urban in nature.

Blacks were flooding into the Northern cities anyway, looking for economic opportunity. They were breaking free of the bonds of church and community in the South, and they wanted to be entertained. Black theatres, nightclubs, and bars opened, and all those establishments required entertainers.

Prohibition, in the 20's and '30's, only led to an even more booming illegal trade in alcohol. "Speakeasies," illicit nightclubs and gambling institutions had the additional draw of danger and lawlessness, that universal appeal of living on the edge. Black musicians began to play these clubs, too, even those catering to white audiences.

Meanwhile, in the South, black musicians and black partiers were gathering in "juke joints" or "barrelhouses," rented shacks with basically no amenities where people gathered to drink, play, dance, and listen to music.

Along with the men, women began to play in these venues. Many of them had started out playing in church, and many were very young runaways lured by the music business. After all, there were very few attractive job prospects for black women. They could be wives, totally dependent on their men, or they could be maids or washerwomen. A woman who wanted more, who craved some independence, had to look for it in unconventional ways.

Music was one of those ways.

Of course, this was a hard-drinking, hard-loving, hard-fighting life, and a woman had to be tough. Many of the women blues singers were tall, big-boned, and quick with temper and fist. All of them could stand up for themselves. There were no shrinking violets among the early blues women.

The entire early history of the blues took place in a time of strict segregation. Black musicians could not eat in the same restaurants, shop in the same stores, use the same rest rooms, or stay in the same hotels as whites. They were often stopped and harassed by police as they traveled from place to place.

In an article on Memphis Minnie, Del Rey points out:

"In 1907 a blues musician played in all kinds of places: house parties, barrel houses, work camps, traveling shows. It's hard to imagine how prevalent live music was before the advent of consumer electronics. Anywhere you hear canned music now would probably have had a live musician--well, maybe not elevators. Sometimes a blues musician got paid with an apple or a can of sardines, sometimes (she) made as much as a hundred dollars."(1)

Things didn't change much for years.

Conditions, even into the 50's, were often very harsh for these musicians. Ruth Brown spoke of traveling in the 50's in interviews, and described bathing with rubbing alcohol and dressing in parking lots by the light from the car's headlights, and eating at the back doors of greasy spoons and in alleys behind restaurants.

Performers often worked six nights a week, and many of these jobs were one night only. They would travel all night in cars and broken down buses, with no heat or air conditioning, or on trains to get to the next stop, and then take off to do it again. They developed a system of black families with spare bedrooms they could stay with across the country, or stayed in black rooming houses. (2)

It could be a lonely business, so musicians often teamed up and traveled together, and they formed close bonds with one another.

Generally, it was the love of the music and performing, and the lack of any better opportunity, that kept them going. When a performer, like Ma Rainey or Bessie Smith, was able to travel by private train, that was the height of success.

Interestingly, among musicians, there was a lot less prejudice. Musicians tended only to care about the music, and if a person had talent, often that was all that mattered. Black and white musicians often played together, although they seldom traveled together.

And the blues attracted white people as well as black people, especially in the South.

In the South, especially among the poor and lower middle class people, there usually wasn't a lot of difference in lifestyle between blacks and whites. They worked the same sorts of jobs, ate the same kind of food, and had the same kind of money and relationship problems.

Southern people, black and white, understood and responded to the blues, and it was a mixed crowd who often filled the tent shows and, later, the dance halls, although attempts were made to keep the races separate, often without success if the music was really, really good.

Black blues women faced the same problems as the men, and because they were women, they also had to be able to defend themselves against unwanted sexual advances. They were already breaking all kinds of taboos, playing what many people called "devil music," and singing either straight out or through double-talk about sex in places no decent woman would be found. It's not hard to imagine what an easy step it was to break other boundaries, too.

Many of the classic blues women, like Ma Rainey and Bessie Smith, were lesbian or bi-sexual. Most took their affection where they could get it, including what were known as "buffet" clubs, "buffet" because you could get anything you wanted there. As we will see later, many were arrested and spent a few nights here and there for their unorthodox tastes and partying ways.

But they survived, and they played incredible music. That music has outlived the early blues queens, and is being carried on today by a whole new breed of female blues singers, black and white. Here is a look at some of them, old and new.

PART I: The Early Blues Women

Early 1900's to 1960

1. MAMIE SMITH

Mamie Smith was born Mamie Robinson in 1883, in
Cincinnati, Ohio. By most accounts, she wasn't really much
of a blues singer, since she was a vaudeville performer at
heart. She got her start at the age of 10, as a dancer in a
vaudeville act, The Four Dancing Mitchells. She was part
of Salem Tutt Whitney and Homer Tutt's traveling show,
"The Smart Set." With them, she went to New York in
1913, and then quit the show to perform in the lively clubs
around Harlem.(1) In 1918, she appeared onstage in

Perry Bradford's musical, "Made in Harlem." (2) Bradford went on to become instrumental in Mamie's career.

It was in 1920 that Mamie Smith suddenly became very important, even key, to the history of the blues. In that year, she became the first blues singer to record a blues record, for Okeh records. Like many important events in history, it was not planned; the session was supposed to be for Sophie Tucker, but she was sick and Mamie filled in for her.

The songs on that first session were "That Thing Called Love," and "You Can't Keep a Good Man Down," by Perry Bradford. The record sold surprisingly well, so Okeh decided to record Mamie again. The record this time was another song by Perry Bradford "Crazy Blues," and it was wildly successful, selling over a million copies in six months and opening the door for the blues explosion of the 1920's.

It was the first time the recording industry realized there was a market for "race records," and opened the door for the great blues women like Bessie Smith, Big Mama Thornton, Ma Rainey, and all the rest. Never before had a record been advertised specifically as being a "colored' artist, targeted to a "colored" audience.(2)

Throughout the 1920's, Mamie continued to make records for Okeh, and also for the Victor label. She toured the US and Europe with her band, "The Jazz Hounds," in a show with a distinctly vaudeville name: "Mamie Smith's Struttin' Along Review."

During this time period, a number of low-budget films were made featuring black performers. Mamie appeared in a number of them, beginning with an early sound movie called "Jail House Blues," in 1929.

Although she retired from music in 1931, she returned to performing for more movies beginning in 1939 with

Paradise in Harlem. Between 1939 and 1943 she appeared in a number of nearly-forgotten films, such as "Mystery in Swing,"" Sunday Sinners, ""Stolen Paradise, ""Murder on Lenox Avenue," and "Because I Love You."(3)

Mamie Smith died in New York on August 16, 1946, having started something unstoppable and earning her claim to fame. (4)

MAMIE SMITH AND HER JAZZ HOUNDS

An example of early advertising of "Race" records to white audiences.

2. MA RAINEY

"When Ma Rainey

Comes to town

Folks from anyplace

Miles Aroun'

From Cape Girardeau,

Poplar Bluff

Flock in to hear

Ma Do Her Stuff

Comes flivverin' in,

Or ridin' mules,

Or packed in trains,

Picknickin' fools..

That's what it's like

For miles on down

To New Orleans Delta

And Mobile Town,

When Ma Hits Anywhere Around."

- Sterling Brown

Ma Rainey's parents were Thomas and Ella Pritchett, singers and dancers. She claimed to have been born in 1886, but the 1900 census places her birth in 1882. At birth, she was named Gertrude.

Ma began her stage career at age 14 in a revue called "A Bunch of Blackberries" and began touring the vaudeville circuit. In 1902, she married a song and dance man named William Rainey. He was known as "Pa" Rainey, so at that point she became "Ma" Rainey, and they performed as "Rainey and Rainey, Assassinators of the Blues."

They toured all over the country, especially the South, as part of several minstrel shows. One of these shows was The Rabbit Foot Minstrels, where Ma met and became friends with a young Bessie Smith.

By the 1920's, Ma Rainey was the most popular star on the TOBA circuit, but she did not make her first recording until 1923. At that time, she was billed as the "Mother of the Blues." Between 1923 and 1928, during the first heyday of the blues, she recorded more than 100 songs for Paramount. For a while, she was riding high, making good money. By the 1930's, the Depression had hit and the big blues money was over, but Ma continued to work until 1935 when she retired to Columbus, Georgia.

Unlike many of the other great blues women, Ma was a good businesswoman, smart with money, and she bought and managed two theatres and owned her own home. (1)

You can get a taste of what a performance by Ma was like in a recording that is readily available today, "Ma Rainey's Black Bottom," a song based on a popular dance of the 1920's. From Pa's raucous introduction, "And now Ma Rainey's gonna show you her Black Bottom," to the closing notes, the song still captures the strength and sexual provocativeness of Ma Rainey's voice. She must have been something to see.

A description by a contemporary at this time gives us an idea of how spectacular she really was:

"She was an extraordinary-looking woman, ugly-attractive with a short, stubby body, big-featured face and a vividly painted mouth full of gold teeth; she would be loaded down with diamonds--in her ears, round her neck, in a tiara on her head, on her hands, everywhere. Beads and bangles mingled jingling with the frills on her expensive stage gowns. For a time her trademark was a fabulous necklace of gold coins, from 2.50 dollar coins to heavy 20 dollar 'Eagles' with matching gold earrings." (2)

In her personal life, Ma was just as outrageous as she was on stage. She was bisexual, and she didn't hide it, at least not in her music, as in the lyrics to "Prove it On Me,"
Went out last night with a crowd of my friends,
They must have been women, 'cause I don't like no men..."(3)

Further proof that Ma sure did like women came in 1925. Ma was arrested in Columbus, Georgia, when police responded to a call and found her, according to the Ma Rainey page of Lambda.net,

"...in a room full of naked women in "intimate" situations. Rainey spent the night in jail for hosting an "indecent party" and was bailed out the following morning by her friend and fellow blues singer Bessie Smith." (4)

Over the years, there's been a lot of speculation about Ma's relationship with Bessie Smith, who was about 15 when she joined the Rabbit Foot Minstrels. Certainly, Ma took her under her wing professionally and was her mentor and her friend; whether they were more than that in the five years they toured together in the show is anyone's guess. But it does seem significant that it was Bessie who came to the rescue after Ma's arrest.

America was still a deeply racist society for all of Ma's life. This is illustrated by the fact that despite Ma Rainey's vast contributions to American music, her long career, and her successful business career as a theatre owner in the 1930's, when she died in 1939, her obituary in the Columbus, Georgia paper listed her as a "housekeeper."

This "housekeeper" was inducted into the Blues Foundation Hall of Fame in 1983, included in the Rock and Roll Hall of Fame as an "early influence" in 1990, and honored on her own postage stamp in 1994. She would have loved that.

3. BESSIE SMITH

According to the 1910 census, Bessie Smith was born on
April 15, 1894, in Chattanooga, Tennessee. Her mother
was named Laura; her father, William, a part-time minister,
died while she was still a baby. By the time she was nine,
her mother died as well, and her sister, Viola, was left to
raise the family.

The family was desperately poor, and so, at the age of
nine, Bessie and her brother began performing for nickels
and dimes in front of the White Elephant saloon, which was

in the heart of black Chattanooga in those strictly segregated days.

Charlie left home in 1904 to join a traveling troupe, but Bessie had to wait until 1912, when she was hired by the Rabbit Foot Minstrels.

At first, she was hired as a dancer, because Ma Rainey was the featured singer with the troupe, but eventually, Bessie began to sing as well. Ma befriended her and helped her hone her performances.

As mentioned earlier, there has been a great deal of speculation as to whether there was a romantic element to the relationship between Bessie and Ma, but what is known is that they were and remained good friends. (1)

Bessie became a very popular performer in her own right on the TOBA vaudeville circuit throughout the South, but it was only in 1923, during the first heyday of the blues, that she cut her first records for Columbia.

After she began recording, her career really flourished. She became the main headliner for the TOBA circuit, working the theatres in the winter and tent shows in the summer. Eventually, she became the highest paid performer on the circuit, and even had her own railroad car to travel in.

While Ma Rainey was billed as the "Mother of the Blues," Bessie was known as "the Queen of the Blues." (2) She cut about 180 recordings for Columbia, and amazingly, 160 of them are still available on disc today!(3)

At the height of her popularity, Bessie flaunted her good fortune and tantalized her audience by dressing the part of blues royalty, as Mae Barnes tells us in "Wild Women Don't Get the Blues:"

"Bessie used to wear the most fabulous costumes. Birds of paradise all in her hair. Along the sides of her gowns there were feathers sticking out from everywhere. Then she changed and wore evening gowns with beads and rhinestones; they were popular in those days. No sequins, but just beads, beads, loads of beads and rhinestones, big rhinestones."(4)

But those flush times couldn't last. Like the other great blues women of the 20's, Bessie's career was virtually ended by the Depression. No one wanted to hear the blues in the 30's.

She continued to perform in small clubs, however, and in 1933, John Hammond saw her perform in Philadelphia and asked her to cut four sides for Okeh records. These 4 sides, cut in 1933 for $30.00 each, were Bessie's last recordings, and include her classic, "Give Me a Pig's Foot." (5)

In 1937, Bessie Smith was involved in a terrible car crash. She was taken to what was then the black hospital in Clarksdale (now the Riverside Hospital,) where her arm was amputated. However, she never regained consciousness, and died the next day. In a 1937 article in Down Beat magazine, John Hammond claimed that she died as the result of a white hospital's refusal to admit her. This is not true; there is no indication that she was ever taken to any hospital other than the one at which she died, which was less than a mile from the white hospital.

Indeed, she was treated at the accident scene by a white doctor, Dr. Hugh Smith, who worked to save her even after another car crashed into the parked cars, injuring a white couple who also needed his attention. He saw her off to the hospital before turning his attention to that couple. So, there is no truth to the rumor that she died because of neglect from the white establishment, and Hammond withdrew his claim that that was what happened, admitting he was misinformed.

However, this story resulted in a popular play, *The Death of Bessie Smith*, by Edward Albee. (6)

Bessie had a big personality to match her big voice. Here is what the owner of the Apollo Theatre said about her:

"She was a difficult and temperamental person, she had her love affairs, which frequently interfered with her work, but she never was a real problem. Bessie was a person for whose artistry, at least, I had the profoundest respect. I don't ever remember any artist in all my long, long years -- and this goes back to some of the famous singers, including Billie Holiday -- who could evoke the response from her listeners that Bessie did. Whatever pathos there is in the world, whatever sadness she had, was brought out in her singing -- and the audience knew it and responded to it."(7)

Physically, Bessie was a big woman; about six foot tall and 200 pounds. She didn't believe in taking anything from anybody and never backed away from a fight. In Bessie, Chris Albertson describes a time when a man was causing trouble with the females at a party, and Bessie knocked him down. Later, the man retaliated by stabbing her in an alley. She returned to the stage the next day against doctor's orders. (7)

Bessie's husband was a man name Jack Gee, and their story is legendary. In an interview on the Jerry Jazz Man website, Chris Albertson, who wrote the definitive biography of Bessie Smith, explains their marriage this way:

"It affected her career because their marriage was such a roller coaster affair. When he was not there, she would go off the deep end and drink a lot, have parties involving sexual liaisons, and so forth. When he would suddenly appear -- and he had a tendency to show up unexpectedly when they were on the road -- she would sober up and wouldn't even want to talk about parties and things. Her marriage gave her life a balance that it obviously needed. But he was so different from her. He never got used to show business, but he liked the money."(8)

While Gee never made any money himself, and came and went from the relationship randomly, Bessie loved him obsessively and constantly bought him expensive presents. She was desperate to keep him in her life, but that did not stop her from taking other lovers to try to fill the gap when he was gone.

In 1926, an episode occurred which summed up the relationship. Bessie discovered that Jack was having an affair with one of her backup singers. She beat the girl up and threw her off the train, then chased Jack down the tracks firing at him with his own handgun. (9)

It was a violent relationship on both sides. Bessie sang:

"It's all about a man who always kicks and dogs me around

It's all about a man who always kicks and dogs me aroun';

And when I try to kill him, that's when my love for him

come down..." (10)

Of course, Bessie had affairs with her chorus girls herself.

Like many of the blues women, she was bisexual. As

Bessie sang, in "T'ain't Nobody's Business If I Do,"

"There ain't nothin' I can do or nothin' I can say,

That folks don't criticize me;

But I'm going to do just as I want to anyway,

and don't care if they all despise me..

If I take a notion,

To jump off in the ocean,

'T'ain't nobody's business if I do.."(11)

When it came to other blues women and her

performances, Bessie was territorial. She didn't want any

other star on any of her shows. For the most part, she refused to record with other blues singers, too, although she did do a few very amusing songs with Clara Smith, in which the two carry on a mock competition. In real life, though, the competition was fierce and not funny, and Bessie alone ruled Bessie's roost. The relationship with Clara Smith ended in a fist fight at a party, which Bessie won. (12)

There were times when Bessie's temper landed her in jail, and other times when she did other unsavory things, like pitching temper tantrums during performances. But life on the road was tough, and a woman had to be tough to make it. Bessie did what she had to do to be a survivor.

In the long run, the music prevailed and outlasted Bessie herself. Janis Joplin was responsible for a great deal of the revival of interest in Bessie's music, as she never failed to take any opportunity to credit her as a huge influence.

After Janis became wildly popular in the 1960's, before her own tragic death, she discovered that Bessie's grave was unmarked, and she wanted to pay for her gravestone. She found out about the unmarked grave when a Philadelphia newspaper started a campaign to mark the grave, and she ended up splitting the cost with another woman, Juanita Green. (13)

Bessie was inducted into the Blues Foundation Hall of Fame in 1996, and into the Rock and Roll Hall of Fame as an "early influence" in 1989.

4. IDA COX

Ida Cox was born in 1896 in Toccoa, Georgia. Her birth name was Ida Prather. As a child, she sang in the church choir. In 1910, at the age of 14, she ran away from home to join a traveling minstrel show. Sometime in the 1910's, she married Adler Cox, also a member of the traveling show. In addition to singing, Ida also performed as a comedienne. Also about this time, she performed with Jelly Roll Morton for a while.(1)

Then, in 1923, Ida signed a recording contract with Paramount Records, who promoted her as the "Uncrowned

Queen of the Blues." (Bessie Smith already had the title of "Queen of the Blues.") (2) At Paramount, she recorded her best-known song and an anthem for women everywhere: "Wild Women Don't Get the Blues:"

"You never get nothing by being an angel child
You better change your ways and get real wild
I wanna tell you something, I wouldn't tell you a lie
Wild women are the only kind that really get by

'Cause wild women don't worry, wild women don't have
their blues.."(3)

Like Ma Rainey, Ida Cox was no fool when it came to her money. She acted as her own agent and manager, and she had a financially successful career. Unlike most of the blues singers, she managed to keep performing and even occasionally performing throughout the Depression. (4)

In 1939, at Carnegie Hall, Ida performed in a John Hammond production called "From Spirituals to Swing," a rare, integrated performance, which sold out.

Ida Cox was still performing in 1945, when she had a stroke. After that, she sang exclusively in her church choir until 1961, when she made' Blues from Rampart Street,' her last recording. She died of cancer in 1967, but her legacy continues. (5) Hardly a female singer today has not recorded "Wild Women" at some time or other.

5. SISTER ROSETTA THARPE

"I hear Rosetta singing in the night

Echos of light that shines like stars after they're

gone…"

  - "Sister Rosetta Goes Before Us," Alison Krause

Sister Rosetta Tharpe was born in 1921 in Cotton

Plant, Arkansas. Her mother was a traveling

missionary and gospel singer and Tharpe developed a

unique style based on the Gospel "shouters" of the day. At seventeen, she was signed to Decca records and began a highly successful career, playing both secular and gospel music. She was one of the first successful crossovers from gospel to popular music.

Among Tharpe's hits were "This Train," now a perennial folk music favorite, and "Rock Me," by Georgia Tom Dorsey, another artist with one foot planted in the "light" of gospel music and one in the "dark" of the blues. Based on these successful songs, she began to perform with popular acts like Cab Calloway and Benny Goodman.

In 1944, Sister Rosetta began recording with boogie-woogie pianist Sammy Price and recorded a song called "Strange Things Happen Every Day" which reached the Top Ten on the race records charts.

After the end of World War II, Decca teamed Rosetta with Marie Knight. They recorded "Up Above My Head,"

"Up above my head
I hear music in the air
And I really do believe
There's a Heaven somewhere. . ."

Like her other songs, the combination of a strong, positive gospel message and a bouncy, infectious melody made "Up Above My Head" a commercial success.

However, in the 1950's, an attempt to record completely secular blues alienated many of Tharpe's core fans in the gospel community, who considered the blues to be "the Devil's music." She eventually returned to the gospel scene, but her popularity had peaked.

Like many other blues performers of the day, Sister Rosetta saw something of a renewal of her fortunes during the folk boom of the early 60's. In 1964, she toured the UK with Reverend Gary Smith, Muddy Waters, and others who have become blues legends.

Sister Rosetta continued to perform until 1970, when she had a stroke and lost a leg to the ravages of diabetes. She died in 1973 as a result of complications of the disease. At that time, she was buried in Philadelphia in an unmarked grave. It was not until after her induction into the Blues Hall of Fame in 2007 that renewed interest in her career led to a concert to raise funds for a gravestone, which was finally placed in 2008.

Despite her relative obscurity today, Sister Rosetta Tharpe profoundly influenced such musicians as Elvis Presley and Johnny Cash, Little Richard and Aretha

Franklin. A new generation of fans will know her name due to the 2007 hit recording by Robert Plant and Alison Kraus quoted at the beginning of this chapter, "Sister Rosetta Goes Before Us."

6. VICTORIA SPIVEY

Victoria Spivey was born in 1906 in Houston, Texas. Her father was a part-time musician and a flagman for the railroad, and her mother was a nurse. At age 12, she started her career playing piano in a movie theater in Houston. Before long, she was also playing and singing in brothels and saloons, and gay hangouts, like most of the blues women of her time.(1)

Sometimes she played alone, but sometimes she played with great blues guitarists like Blind Lemon Jefferson. She was greatly influenced by Ida Cox, and sang the same sort

of sexy, suggestive lyrics that did so well for Ida and for

Sippie Wallace and others. These are the songs that

helped these women make comebacks later in life, when

they so well suited the sexual freedom of the sixties and

seventies. Victoria made her first recording for Okeh

records in 1926, when she was only 20 years old. She

recorded her own songs, including the classic "Black

Snake Blues," and "Dirty Woman Blues," which were best-

sellers for Okeh. For the next few years, her recording

career was hot, and she also worked as a songwriter for a

music publishing company in St. Louis during this period.

Her song, "Organ Grinder," for instance, was recorded by

Ethel Waters as well as by Victoria: (2)

"Organ grinder, organ grinder,

organ grinder, play that melody

Take your organ, and grind some more for me

Grind it north, grind it north,

grind it north, and grind it east and west,

When you grind it slow, I like it the best..." (3)

Victoria was not hit as hard by the Depression as many blues musicians were. She continued to record, moving from Okeh to Victor in 1930. She also started to appear in vaudeville reviews, including the very popular Hellzapoppin' review in New York City, toured with Louis Armstrong and his band, and had small roles in the movie musicals that became popular with the advent of sound in motion pictures in the 30's, such as King Vidor's film, "Hallelujah!" (3)

Ms. Spivey continued to perform until 1951, when she retired from secular music to sing and play in church, as so many did in that time of spiritual revival across the country. However, she returned to the blues in 1961, beginning by recording four songs with an old musical companion, Lonnie Johnson, for his album, "Idle Hours." She followed

this up with a recording, "Songs We Taught Your Mother,"
with Alberta Hunter and Lucille Hegeman. By this time,
Victoria was on her fourth husband. His name was Lyn
Kunstadt, a jazz historian, and with him she started her
own records company, "Spivey Records." Though Spivey
was a small, low-budget company, it recorded many of the
greats, including Alberta Hunter, Luther Johnson, Sippie
Wallace, and Otis Rush. Even Bob Dylan, who had heard
Victoria sing in Greenwich Village, appeared on Spivey
Records, billed

as "Blind Boy Grunt." Janis Ian topped that
by appearing as "Blind Girl Grunt!" (4)
Victoria never retired from music again; she
continued to record for the rest of her life.

She died of natural causes in 1976 and is
buried in Hempstead, New York.(5)

7. ALBERTA HUNTER

"The blues? Why, the blues are a part of me. They're like a chant. The blues are like spirituals, almost sacred. When we sing blues, we're singing out our hearts, we're singing out our feelings. Maybe we're hurt and just can't answer back, then we sing or maybe even hum the blues. When I sing, 'I walk the floor, wring my hands and cry -- Yes, I walk the floor, wring my hands and cry,'... what I'm doing is letting my soul out." --Alberta Hunter (1)

Alberta Hunter was born in 1895 in Memphis Tennessee. She ran away from home at the age of 12, with the intention of becoming a singer.

Times were hard at first, but in 1911 she had her professional debut at a bordello called Dago Frank's on Chicago's South Side, where she was successful enough to stay until 1913, when a murder closed the club down. She quickly found work in another club.

About this time, she married briefly, but according to Red Hot Jazz, she never consummated her marriage and, was, in truth, a lesbian. Shortly after her husband moved out for good, she met a woman named Lottie Taylor, who became her lover. The two stayed together for years. (2)

By 1915, Alberta was well known around Chicago, still playing the tough clubs and becoming a local star.

Chicago was a wild town for the entertainment scene, and during one performance Alberta's piano player was shot and killed onstage! (3)

In 1921, Alberta decided it was time to move on and try her luck in New York. She explained why in a song:

"Folk's I ain't got a crying penny, my poor feet on the ground,

And if I ever want to be somebody I sho'got to leave this town…"(4)

In New York, she signed with Black Swan records, which later merged with Paramount.   According to the VH1 website, she also recorded for other labels at this time, under various pseudonyms, including Alberta Prime and Anna Jones. Often, her performances were backed by famous black musicians of the time, including Louis Armstrong, Fats Waller, Eubie Blake, and Fletch Henderson. She cut over 80 sides in the 20's, mostly before 1925.

Aside from her success as a singer, Alberta Hunter wrote some notable songs that were covered by other blues singers, including "Downhearted Blues," a major hit for Bessie Smith.

Because of her huge success, Alberta was able to tour overseas, and beginning in 1927, she spent an extended time in London, which kept her from suffering during the Depression like most of the blues singers of her time.

When she returned to the US in 1935, however, things did not go so well. She had a number of recording sessions, but no hits. By the 40's, she was working for small recording companies like Juke Box. Still, she performed at the 1940 World's Fair and soon was working the USO circuit during World War II. As a live performer, she remained very popular. (5)

Alberta never stopped performing until 1956, when she retired from the music business. In her 60's, she became a licensed practical nurse, and no one she worked with knew about her music career. Only once, in 1961, did she step back into the musical world, to make a recording for Bluesville with Lovie Austin and Lil Harden Armstrong.

In 1977, at the age of 81, Alberta retired from nursing. But was she ready to sit back and relax? No, she was ready to go back on the road! Between 1977 and her death in 1984, Alberta found a whole new generation of fans with four down and dirty recordings for Columbia records.

From the bordellos to international stardom, from a teenager to an octogenarian, Alberta Hunter made her own way and sang her songs. Unlike most of the other blues women, she lived a long life and died a natural death. She said,

""I'm not living the blues; I'm just singing for the women

who think they can't speak out. Can't a man alive mistreat

me, 'cause I know who I am."(6)

8. **MEMPHIS MINNIE**

Memphis Minnie was born Lizzie Douglas in Algiers, Louisiana, on June 3, 1897. She started playing guitar at age 7, and is as well-known as a pioneering blues guitarist as she is as a blues singer. As a child, she played parties around Algiers, billed as "Kid Douglas." At thirteen, she ran away to Memphis and started playing in the clubs and for tips on Beale Street.(1)

The next year, she joined the Ringling Brothers Circus. She toured with them throughout the 1910's and early

'20's, and it was at this time that she began to be called "Memphis Minnie." (2)

A flamboyant character, Minnie "wore bracelets made of silver dollars," (3) and "would spit tobacco wearing a chiffon ball gown." (4) She was greatly influenced by Ma Rainey, and liked to flash a luxurious lifestyle just as Ma did.

In the early 1920's, Minnie moved in with and may or may not have married Casey Bill Weldon, a guitarist with the very popular Memphis Jug Band. But by 1929, she had definitely moved on to another guitar man, Joe McCoy, and we know that she did marry him. They were playing in a Memphis barber shop when a scout for Columbia records invited them to record in New York. Minnie had just turned 32 when they made their first recording for Columbia. They recorded together as Memphis Minnie and Kansas Joe until 1935, when they broke up.

Minnie continued to record, both alone and with a number of bluesmen, in Chicago and in Memphis. She married again, to a man named Ernest Lawlers, better known as "Little Sun Joe." She kept on recording, with and without her husband, right up until 1958, when poor health forced her to retire. (5)

Minnie was one of the first blues musicians to play electric guitar, embracing the new technology in the early 1940's. She was a great guitar player. In his autobiography, Big Bill Broonzy describes a contest between him and Memphis Minnie in Chicago. This was in 1933, when Bill was enormously popular. Minnie beat him, and the judges awarded her a bottle of whiskey and a bottle of gin. Bill confiscated half the prize, the whiskey, and slid under a table to drink it as two of the judges hoisted Minnie to their shoulders, much to the disapproval of jealous Joe McCoy. Bill did not hold a grudge; he and Minnie became good friends and often performed together in the years following his defeat. (6)

Minnie, by all accounts, could drink and party and play guitar just as good as any bluesman of her time. She loved jewelry and fine clothes, and she loved whiskey and tobacco, too. She recorded over four decades, hundreds of sides, and influenced many other singers, male and female.

Although a heart attack in 1957 and the poor health of Little Son Joe (who was her partner for over 23 years,) forced her to retire in 1957, Minnie lived to see the revived interest in her music in the late 1960's and 1970's. In 1971, her song, "When the Levee Breaks," was recorded by Led Zeppelin, with a different tune and a few altered lyrics. Minnie died in 1973, and was inducted into the Blues Foundation Hall of fame in 1980. (7)

9. SIPPIE WALLACE

Sippie Wallace was born Beulah Thomas in Houston, Texas in 1898. Her daddy was a deacon in the Baptist church, and as a child she sang and played piano in church.

But she and her siblings were fascinated with the tent shows that came through town, and by the time she was in her mid teens, she was singing in those shows with her brothers, traveling all over Texas. In 1915, she moved to New Orleans and married a man named Matt Wallace. In the 1920's, she began touring on the TOBA circuit, and was billed as "The Texas Nightingale."

In 1923, she followed her brothers to Chicago, where she began recording with Okeh records. By 1929, she had recorded over 60 songs for them, most of them written by herself or by her brothers.(1) She had a sassy, raunchy, style that was purely Texas. Not for her, those brooding ballads of love lost and how her man done her wrong! Instead, she sang:

"I'm a real tight woman
I'm a jack of all trades
I can be yo' sweet woman n' also be yo' slave
I can do things so good
'Till you will swear that I have a halo over me..."(2)

And her repertoire also included titles like, "You Got to Know How," and "Jelly Roll Blues." Sippie was hot, and she sounded like a handful.

When the blues rage ended in the 1930's, Sippie temporarily retired from music. During the 1940's and 1950's, she made a few recordings, but she didn't really resume her career until the blues revival days of the 1960's, when her friend blueswoman Victoria Spivey convinced Sippie to make a record with her. After that, Sippie made her own new record, Sippie Wallace Sings the Blues. (3)

In 1970, Sippie suffered a stroke, but she didn't stop performing. She had been a huge influence on contemporary blues woman Bonnie Raitt. Bonnie befriended Sippie, performed with her live, and worked with her on an album, Sippie, which was nominated for a Grammy in 1983 when Sippie was 85 years old, and won the W.C.Handy award for best blues album in 1984.

In those late years, Sippie still maintained her wit and her sassy style. With Bonnie, she sang, "Woman Be Wise:"

"Woman, be wise,

Keep your mouth shut,

Don't advertise your man…"(4)

And you could imagine that if you weren't careful, this woman in her 80's really might could steal your man.

Sippie was never ashamed of her music, even though in later years she also sang and played gospel music. She said, in an interview shortly before her death in 1986,

"I play for a church right now. . . . You don't see any place in the Bible that says you'll go to hell if you sing the blues. If you can sing gospel, you can sing the blues. The only thing that divides the blues from the gospel are the words.

Where you say 'Lord' in gospel, in blues you say 'Daddy.'"

(5)

10. BIG MAMA THORNTON

Big Mama Thornton was born in Montgomery, Alabama in 1926. Her father was a minister and her mother sang in the church choir. As a child, she taught herself to play the drums and the harmonica, and at age 14, she ran away from home to sing with a traveling show, Sammy Green's "Hot Harlem Revue." She was a mountain of a woman: over 6 ft tall and more than 350 pounds, and she had a powerful voice to match her size.

In 1948, Big Mama left the Hot Harlem Revue to play clubs in Texas. From there, she gradually found audiences around the country.

In 1952, she played the Apollo in Harlem as a headliner, and it was an audience member who coined the name, "Big Mama." It suited her, and it stuck. It was around this time that she was discovered by Don Robey, a black club and record store owner in Houston. It was he who first put Big Mama on record. (1)

The first recording Robey made with Thornton was the work of a couple of young white songwriters, Jerry Leiber and Mike Stoller. They wrote a perfect song for Big Mama, showcasing her ferocious style and trademark growl. The name of the song was "Hound Dog," and in 1951, it hit Number 1 on the Billboard Rhythm and Blues charts for 9 straight weeks. Unfortunately for Big Mama Thornton's career, not long after that, in 1956, a major star of the new rock 'n roll craze named Elvis Presley, recorded "Hound

Dog," and after that it was forever associated with Presley and not with Big Mama. (2)

Ironically, before Elvis, Big Mama's recording of "Hound Dog," backed by "They Call Me Big Mama," had sold nearly two million copies. In an unfortunate sign of the times, Big Mama received one check for the record, for a mind-bending $500. (3)

Blues music was still a rough business in the '50's, and it took a tough woman like Big Mama to survive it. In 1978, Charles Sawyers interviewed Big Mama (referred to in the story by her real name, Willie Mae,) and she told him about the time Johnny Ace shot himself in her dressing room:

"… Johnny was sitting with girlfriend Olivia on his lap, waving his pistol around, pointing it at Willie Mae. "Don't snap that on me," she told him. Johnny grinned and put the gun to Olivia's head. "Stop that, Johnny, you'll git someone killed," Willie Mae shouted at him. "Nothin' to worry about,"

Johnny replied, coolly, "ain't but one bullet here and I know

exactly where it is." He turned the gun on himself, put it to

his

temple and pulled the trigger. And that was that. It was

Christmas Eve, 1954, in Houston, Texas."(4)

Just another day on tour for a blueswoman in the '50's.

For some years, Big Mama was restricted to touring what

was known as the "chitlin' circuit" throughout the south,

until the rebirth of interest in the blues in the 1960's

brought her back to the limelight. Her own return to fame

was mainly due to Janis Joplin, who recorded her classic,

"Ball and Chain," and never failed to credit it to Big Mama

when she performed it on nearly every show:

"Sitting down by my window,

Oh, looking at the rain.

S-sitting down by my window now now,

All around I felt it,

All I could see was the rain.

Something grabbed a hold of me, honey,

Felt to me honey like, lord, a ball and chain."(5)

Since everything was happening in San Francisco in the sixties, Big Mama moved there from Houston. From that time until her death, she was a tour fixture.

She played the Monteray Jazz Festival throughout the late sixties and the seventies. Her rough, uninhibited style suited the times and audiences loved her. Many companies, including Arhoolie and Vanguard, recorded her during this time. Even in later years, in 1983, she played the Newport Jazz Festival with Muddy Waters, B.B. King, and Eddie "Cleanhead" Vinson.

Big Mama was found dead by a medical team in a rooming house in Los Angeles on July 25, 1984, a sad ending for a great blues legend. She was inducted into the Blues Foundation Hall of Fame that same year. (6)

11. **RUTH BROWN**

In the 1950's, Ruth Brown was known as "Miss Rhythm," and, as reported on VH1, Atlantic Records was often referred to at that time as "the house that Ruth built." (1)

She was born Ruth Weston in 1928 in Portsmouth, Virginia. Her father was a dockhand and a church choir director. In the 1940's, the teenaged Ruth sang at USO's and in nightclubs, and in 1945 she ran away from home with a trumpeter named Jimmy Brown, marrying him soon after. But eighteen months later, she discovered that her eighteen-year-old husband was already married, and the marriage was annulled. It was the beginning of a long string of unsuccessful relationships, which led Ruth to later joke, "I can pick a good song, but I could never pick a good man." Eventually, she ended up a single mom with two sons. (2)

There were some tough times in her career, too. After a month long gig with Lucky Millander's orchestra in 1947, she was left stranded in Washington, DC after she was fired for bringing the band a round of drinks.

Fortunately, Cab Calloway's sister, Blanche, took in an interest in the young songbird and gave her a gig in her nightclub. Very soon, she became Ruth's manager, and shortly after that a deejay introduced her to Ahmet Ertegun and Herb Abramson, who were just launching Atlantic records in 1948, and Ruth's career appeared to be on the rise.

But just as things seemed to be about to take an upswing for Ruth, she ended up in the hospital for nine months after a very serious car accident. She wasn't able to cut her first record with Atlantic, a ballad called "So Long," until May 1949. Luckily, after such a long string of bad luck, the song was a hit on the Rhythm and Blues charts.

By 1953, Ruth had already had a string of hits on the R & B charts. In that year, she cut the classic, "Mama, He Treats Your Daughter Mean," which brought her much wider attention. Throughout the 50's, she continued to record successful records for a total of 22 hits on the R & B charts, and she attracted audiences not only of black fans, but white fans, too.

In those days of segregation, when Ruth would perform in venues that allowed dancing, the officials would put a rope down the middle of the floor, with blacks on one side and whites on the other. Ruth said,

"I'm overjoyed to say that many times the ropes came down, they'd fall because the music got in the way of attitudes and feelings and nobody cares who rubbed against each other. Everybody was having a good time.

They didn't care what color your face was, for a moment...while the music was good."(3)

Unfortunately, in 1960, Ruth's career faded. Even more unfortunately, by the time she left Atlantic in 1961, she had never received any royalties for all those hit records. She got $69 a side for each one, eventually working her way up to $359 a record. That's all she got, no matter how much money the record made. It was standard for the time. (4)

Throughout the 60's, Ruth was almost forgotten. She worked as a domestic, drove a bus, and raised her children, but in the 70's, like many another blues woman, she began to find her musical career again. It was at this point that her work took even more of a turn toward blues and jazz. She started finding work in clubs. In 1985, John Waters chose her for the role of Motormouth Mabel in "Hairspray," and Ruth was back for good. Havin been discovered by a new medium, in 1989, she starred on Broadway in "Black and Blue," and won a Tony Award.

During the 1980's and 1990's, Ruth made a number of records for Fantasy, and appeared on National Public Radio regularly for Harlem Hit Parade and BluesStage.

At last, it was time for Ms. Brown to stand up for herself. She became involved in a grueling battle with Atlantic records during the 1990's. The fight went on for 9 years as Ruth tried to get the royalties due her for all those hits. Her experience led to the formation of the nonprofit Rhythm and Blues Organization, which fights for the rights of artists who have never gotten their fair share. Among other achievements, they helped acquire past royalty checks for 35 Rhythm and Blues artists from Atlantic records. (5)

In 1993, Ruth Brown was inducted into the Rock and Roll Hall of Fame.
She continued to perform until she suffered a heart attack in 2006, which led to her eventual death in November,

2006. (6) But she had changed the world for herself and many of her blues fellow blues musicians.

As for the impact of her music, her good friend, Charles Brown, with whom she often traveled, summed it up nicely: "Like Bonnie Raitt says, me and Ruth are the Adam and Eve of rhythm and blues." (7)

And so they were.

Part II: BLUES WOMEN FROM THE 60's TO THE PRESENT

BLUES WOMEN TODAY

In the 60's, blues lost popularity for a while. But thanks to English rock musicians, by the late 60's, the style was reviving. Before long, new blues women were emerging, and the style is still going strong today. Here is a look at some of the new breed of blues women, starting with the woman who probably best personified the blues for the late '60's and early 70's, Janis Joplin.

12. **JANIS JOPLIN**

Janis wanted to be the living embodiment of Bessie Smith.
She tried to act tough and free, but she was really
vulnerable and insecure. She loved her Southern Comfort
and she preached free love, but a world of pain came
through in her voice.

She was born on January 19, 1943, in Port Arthur, Texas,
and she tragically died on October 4, 1970, at age 27. In

between, she became the greatest blues singer of her generation. As a teenager, she considered herself a beatnik, and she deliberately set out to copy the style of her idol, Bessie Smith.

For a small woman, she had a huge voice, and she could belt out the blues with the best of them. She played the coffeehouses and the then-popular hootenannies around Texas, but socially, she never fit in in her hometown, and she felt shunned.

After graduating high school in 1960, Janis went off for a brief stint at the University of Texas in Austin. But she didn't feel at home there, either, and in 1963, she headed for San Francisco, living first in North Beach and then settling in Haight Ashbury, which was not yet the center of hippie culture it was to shortly become.

Even though it was not yet the heyday of the drug culture, it was at about this time that Janis began using heroin occasionally, a habit that continued throughout the rest of her short life. She was also drinking heavily and beginning to be known for the love of Southern Comfort that would become legendary.

In 1965, Janis gave in to her need for approval and tried one final time to reform herself. She returned to Port Arthur, tried to dress and act conservatively, and entered Lamar University in Beaumont, Texas. But it didn't last; no matter how hard she tried, Janis just could not be ordinary. The part of her nature that made her the great blues performer she was refused to be denied. So she went back to performing.

By 1966, Janis had come to the attention of a psychedelic rock band known as Big Brother and the Holding Company, and she joined them and returned to Haight-Ashbury, just in time for the infamous "Summer of Love." She made her first public appearance with Big Brother at the mecca of the psychedelic world, Avalon Ballroom, on

June 10, 1966. Not long after that, she and the group signed a deal with an independent records company, Mainstream, and recorded the Big Brother and the Holding Company album. Things looked good, but the singles from the album went basically nowhere so the album's release was indefinitely delayed.

It was only after Janis and Big Brother and the Holding Company made a huge splash at the Monterey Pop Festival in 1967 that the album was finally released. It featured Janis's classic take on Big Mama Thornton's "Ball and Chain," in which it seemed that Janis would tear her heart, and her throat, out. Janis turned into a star almost overnight. For the next two years, her popularity continued to grow, and more and more, the guys in the band became just her backup. But they continued to tour as a group, and in 1968, their second album,
Cheap Thrills, was released. That album, and the film of the Monterey Pop Festival released that year, made Janis into a blues goddess for an entire generation. When she

sang "Piece of My Heart," the emotion was as raw, as painful, and at the same time as exhilarating, as any blues performance has ever been.

By this time, Janis had obviously outgrown her group, and she left them after a benefit performance for the Family Dog on December 1, 1968. She formed a new backup group, The Kozmic Blues Band, and played Woodstock with them in 1969.

Her album with The Kozmic Blues Band, *I Got Them Ol' Kozmic Blues Again, Mama!* went gold, but she never formed the bond with them that she had had with Big Brother, and they broke up after a year, in December 1969.

In 1970, Janis formed another new band, The Full Tilt Boogie Band, and made a valiant attempt to get clean and sober. In September, she started recording a new album, which was to become Pearl. This album included Janis's wryly funny, "Oh, Lord, Won't You Give Me a Mercedes

Benz," and a great version of Kris Kristoferson's "Me and Bobby McGee." Unfortunately, Janis died before the album was released and, at least in this lifetime, could not know that it became her biggest hit ever.

In August of 1970, Janis returned home for her 10th high school reunion. She had high hopes for it, according to interviews at the time, looking forward to showing people that she had succeeded despite their disapproval. But the people in her hometown did not care about her talent and her success; they just thought she was weird. Despite of everything, she was still shunned by her former high school acquaintances.

Two months later, on October 3, 1970, Janis's manager found her dead from a heroin overdose, on the floor at the Landmark Motor Hotel in Los Angeles. She had been distraught when her boyfriend of the time didn't show up for a date. Not even the adulation of an entire generation could fill her need for love and give her the security she needed. Only her beloved Southern Comfort and heroin could fill the void. She was cremated, and her ashes were scattered over the ocean. There was no public funeral or official memorial service, at the request of the family.

In a time when rock music was dominated by males, Janis fused rock and blues to create a sound like no other of the time. She constantly gave credit to Bessie Smith as her idol and inspiration, and she helped to spark the rebirth of interest in the blues women who went before her. She even helped, as we saw in the chapter on Bessie Smith, to see that Bessie got the grave marker she deserved.

As for Janis's memorial, ironically, Port Arthur, the town that never accepted her and caused her such lifelong insecurity created a Janis Joplin memorial in 1988, with a bronze sculpture of their hometown girl.

In 1995, Janis was inducted into the Rock and Roll Hall of Fame, and she also received a lifetime achievement award in 2005.

If there had only been more lifetime, imagine what her achievement could have been. As it is, she stands with Bessie Smith and Ma Rainey as the greatest of the great.

13. **ETTA JAMES**

Etta James actually began her career in the fifties, but she had her main success in the sixties, beginning with the enormous hit, "At Last," in 1961, and she continues to be an active and highly successful performer to this day.

She was born Jamesetta Hawkins, to an unmarried 16-year-old, on January 25, 1938. She started out, like many blues singers, singing gospel in church, but in 1954, at age 16, she took the name Etta James and embarked on her career. Typically, she began on a controversial note. Singer Hank Ballard had a hit called "Work With Me, Annie,' and Etta recorded a hard rocking answer song, "Roll With Me, Henry." But that title was way too suggestive for 1954, so the title was changed to "Dance With Me, Henry." The way Etta sang it, though, it might as well have stayed "Roll with me." Record buyers loved it, and when she followed it up in 1955 with "Good Rockin' Daddy," her career was set. (1)

In 1960, Etta began recording with Chess records, and in 1961 "At Last" hit the R and B charts at #2 and made it all the way to #22 on the pop charts. It became her signature song, and today is as popular as it ever has been. It still is played at weddings, proms, and every other type of occasion that calls for a romantic tune delivered with feeling.

In 1967, Ms. James penned and recorded one of her most popular and still best-known songs, "I'd Rather Go Blind (Blind Girl)":

Something told me it was over
when I saw you and her talking,
Something deep down in my soul said, ´Cry Girl´,
when I saw you and that girl, walking out.
I would rather, I would rather go blind boy,
Than to see you, walk away from me, chile.
Oooo, so you see, I love you so much
That I don't want to watch you leave me baby,
Most of all, I just don't, I just don't want to be free no…(2)

But by the time "I'd Rather Go Blind" was released, Etta was battling heroin addiction. It was a fight that went on for years, until 1974, and sometimes she was sidelined for months at a time. But she stayed with Chess until 1975, and despite some uneven performances she persevered, with another hit, "Tell Mama," in 1967 that's as strong as any of her earlier work.

Even after the Chess years ended in 1975, she continued to record for many labels, including Atlantic. Much of Etta's personal life has been tragic, but she has never stopped recording, and she still wows audiences today, at 69. She's a fighter and a survivor; at one point she gained so much weight that she was over 400 pounds; she had gastric bypass surgery and lost over 200 pounds. (3)

Etta's contributions to music cross many boundaries. She has been recognized by The Blues Foundation, the Rock and Roll Hall of Fame, and The Rockabilly Hall of Fame. She received a Lifetime Grammy Achievement Award in 2003, and in 2004 she was included in Rolling Stone Magazine's "100 Greatest Artists of All Time."

Etta has said:

"I wanna show that gospel, country, blues, rhythm and blues, jazz, rock 'n' roll are all just really one thing. Those are the American music and that is the American culture."(4)

She has done that.

For years, she's been known for her wildly entertaining, often rather "adult" shows. About that, she's been quoted as saying:

"They said that Etta James is still vulgar. I said, Oh, how dare them say I'm still vulgar. I'm vulgar because I dance in the chair. What would they want me to do? Want me to just be still or something like that? I've got to do something."(5)

Etta is vulgar in the same way that blues is vulgar: she reaches way down to the basics of human emotion, and she sings and performs from that basic place in all of us. And in that way, she touches and unites us all.

14. **BONNIE RAITT**

Bonnie Raitt has had a happier fate than many blues singers before her. She is still performing and recording after over thirty years in the business, and her career has never faltered yet. She's won 9 Grammy awards, and she worked hard for every one of them.

She deserves a lot of credit not only for her music but for the way she has gone out of her way to honor her fellow blues musicians, and for taking many a nearly-forgotten legend on tour with her, helping to keep them in the public eye and working to see that they get the financial support they deserve.

Bonnie Raitt was born in 1949 in Burbank, California. Her father was the popular broadway musical star, John Raitt. She began playing guitar at an early age. In her career, she's become known for her proficiency at bottleneck guitar, a favorite style of the classic male blues singers that has not attracted a lot of other women.

Bonnie is not your traditional image of a blues woman. She is white and her family was Quaker. Her father, as we've mentioned, was a Broadway star. But the blues does not depend on the color of one's skin or one's background. She was meant to play the blues, and so she and the blues found each other.

She was a student at Harvard in the sixties, majoring in African studies and planning a career in social activism, when she met Dick Waterman, a blues promoter. Her parents weren't too thrilled when they became close friends; he was 65 years old and she was still a teenager. But, she says," I was amazed by his passion for the music and the integrity with which he managed the musicians."

And through Waterman, she met and befriended many local musicians and became part of the local blues community; so much so that, when Waterman decided to relocate to Philadelphia a year later with many of the musicians he was managing, Bonnie decided to take a break from college and went along.

In Philadelphia, Bonnie started performing with Sippie Wallace, Mississippi Fred McDowell, and other blues legends she had met through Waterman. She fit in so well that in 1970 she caught the attention of a reporter from Newsweek, who started spreading the word about this extraordinary young white girl who sang the blues and played a mean guitar.

This was the beginning of a rebirth of interest in the blues, and record companies started coming around. In 1971, Bonnie accepted a recording offer from Warner Brothers.

With Warner Brothers, she recorded her first album, the self-titled *Bonnie Raitt*, which got warm reviews but didn't excite much attention from the record-buying public. With *Give it Up*, in 1972, and, in 1973, her reviews got even more enthusiastic, and she began to build a cult audience, but commercially she was still not well-known.

It was not until 1977, with *Sweet Forgiveness*, a much more commercial and less gritty album, that Bonnie achieved success with the public. Her cover of Del Shannon's "Runaway," was a hit, and that song remained her biggest commercial success for a long time.

Raitt was better known, possibly, in the 1970's for her political activism; she created the MUSE (Musicians United for Safe Energy) Organization, which spawned a great

Madison Square Garden concert, a three-volume album, and a feature movie, called No Nukes.

But, while Bonnie had a loyal base of fans, commercially she was still not performing as well as Warner Brothers wanted. In 1983, the label decided to make a drastic change, and it dropped her, along with other major artists such as Van Morrison and Arlo Guthrie. Bonnie continued to perform, however, and to be politically active, appearing at Farm Aid and at concerts for Amnesty International.

During this time, like many of her generation, Bonnie also struggled briefly with alcohol and substance abuse issues, but before the 80's were out, she was clean and sober.

After years of stellar but not very successful work, Bonnie finally hit the big time with *Nick of Time*, released in 1989. The album went to the top of the charts and won three Grammy awards. Recorded with producer Don Was, it was her first Number 1 record. Her next album, Luck of the

Draw, one three more awards in 1991, and in 1994,

Longing in Their Hearts added two more to her store.

As Bonnie's success increased she did not forget her old friends. She took Sippie Wallace on tour with her, and many other blues greats, and continues to do so to this day.

She continues to be politically active. And she still plays a mean bottleneck guitar.

15. IRMA THOMAS

Irma Thomas is well-known as "The Soul Queen of New Orleans." She was born Irma Lee in 1941 in Ponchatula, Louisiana, but she was raised in New Orleans. Like many a blues woman before her, as a teenager she sang gospel music. But at 14, she got pregnant and, in accord with the custom of the day, was forced to drop out of school and marry the father of her child. By the age of 17, she was divorced and the mother of two. Before the age of twenty, she married her second husband, Andrew Thomas and had two more children. Then this marriage, too, ended, but she kept the name Thomas. Two failed marriages and four children by the time she was barely out of her teens did not seem to be a surefire recipe for a musical career, although it certainly was enough to acquaint her with the blues.

But Irma had talent and the good luck to be discovered by bandleader Tommy Ridgely. In 1959, she was working as a waitress in a club in New Orleans. She asked if she could sing with the band when they played the club, and they agreed. Irma was fired for not waiting tables, but her singing career was launched. Her very first recording, "You Can Have My Husband (But Please Don't Mess With My Man,") reached #22 on the R and B charts.

In 1964, Irma had her biggest hit on Imperial records, with a song called "I Wish Someone Would Care,"

Sitting home alone

thinking about my past

wondering how I made it

and how long it's gonna last

Success has come to lots of them

and a failure is always there

time waits for no one

and I wish, how I wish

someone would care...

"I was really at the low point when I wrote that", she later
related to author Jeff Hannusch in *I Hear You Knockin':
The Sound of New Orleans Rhythm & Blues.*

"I was just looking back at life. I was a 14-year-old mother,
I had three kids when I was 17, and I was on my second
marriage. At the time, I was breaking up with my husband,
because he was giving me a hard time about being on
stage. It was a song from my heart, that's probably why it
sold so well; I really wanted someone to care, to stand
beside me and care."

Irma's songs usually made the charts, but it wasn't the records that made her the Soul Queen. The Rolling Stones did cover one of her songs, "Time is On My Side," but probably very few people realized it was one of hers at the time. She had frustrating stints at Imperial and Chess in the 60's and 70's, and finally drifted back to New Orleans and began performing at "The Lion's Den," a club she opened in 1977 with her manager and husband, Emile Jackson. She was a riveting live performer and very popular around The Big Easy.

In 1986, Irma finally found a record company that knew what to do with her, when she signed with Rounder records. With Rounder, she made a couple of excellent studio albums and then a live record, Live! *Simply the Best*, which got a Grammy nomination in 1991.

In 1998, Irma recorded *Sing It!,* with her long time fan Marcia Ball and blues woman Tracey Nelson. While the album was not a huge hit, it got good reviews and generated several concert performances.

Throughout all the recording ups and downs, Irma continued to perform in New Orleans to fanatical audiences, especially at "The Lion's Den." But when hurricane Katrina devastated New Orleans, it flooded both the club and Irma's home, and she and her husband were forced to temporarily relocate to Gonzales, Louisiana. Inspired by Katrina, in 2006, she recorded her bluesiest album, *After the Rain*. (3)

Today, Irma continues to light up performance venue and fire up audiences, earning her title of "The Soul Queen of New Orleans" over and over again.

16. MARCIA BALL

Marcia Ball was born in Orange, Texas in 1949, but grew up in Vinton, Louisiana. She started playing piano at age 5. At 13, she discovered Irma Thomas, and was introduced to the blues. Marcia says, "She just blew me away, she caught me totally unaware. Once I started my own band, the first stuff I was doing was Irma's."(1) That would have been in 1966, when she started college at Louisiana University and began performing with a blues-rock group called Gum.

After her graduation in 1970, Ball intended to go to San Francisco, but her car broke down in Austin. She fell in love with the city and settled down, beginning to play local clubs with a group called Frieda and the Firedogs. She began to study New Orleans music more intensely, and her keyboard style was strongly influenced by New Orleans piano legend, Professor Longhair.

"Having found this wonderful piano world, it called to me," she has said. "I think one of the reasons that it worked so well for me was that my background in keyboards had been so traditional and old fashioned anyway. My grandmother played, and was a ragtime era piano player, so I grew up with a lot of old sheet music in my ears, old piano songs and styles in my head. It was something that I already felt close to, to hear those New Orleans chord changes - they're not straight blues changes, they're not pop changes, they have a real old fashioned sense to them."(2)

In 1974, Frieda and the Firedogs broke up and Marcia Ball was ready to start her solo career. She recorded first for Capitol records in 1978, but is probably best known for the Rounder records she recorded throughout the 80's and 90's, including *Hot Tamale Baby* and *Let Me Play With Your Poodle.* In 1998, she got the chance to sing with her idol, Irma Thomas, and fellow blues woman Tracey Nelson on an album entitled *Sing It!,* which was nominated for a W.C. Handy award as well as a Grammy.

While these albums are great, Ball is one of those performers who is at her best live. She has played many major festivals and appeared in concert at the White House with B.B.King and Della Reese. She won the W.C. Handy award for Contemporary Female Vocalist of the Year in 1998 and was nominated in that category again in 2000. In 2001, she was nominated for the W.C. Handy award for Best Blues Instrumentalist-Keyboards. In 2002, she won her second W.C. Handy award, this time for Blues

Album of the Year for her Alligator album, *Presumed Innocent.* (3)

Melding Louisiana boogie-woogie swamp music and blues, Marcia keeps the keyboards, and the audiences, rocking. And, like Bonnie Raitt, she honors and enjoys the legends who influenced her, and has featured many of them in her shows. She's been known to do an entertaining noise fest called "Pianofest," in which she plays onstage with five other pianists and a drummer. She has played with Fats Domino and many other New Orleans and Texas legends.

Marcia, with the other women in this book, is truly helping to keep the blues alive in the eyes and ears of fans everywhere.

17. **KATIE WEBSTER**

Katie Webster was born Kathryn Thorne in 1936 in
Houston, Texas. Continuing the Texas/Louisiana blues
link, she became popular in the 1950's and 1960's on the
Louisiana "swamp blues" circuit. Like Marcia Ball, her
boogie-woogie piano playing was a big part of her appeal.

Growing up, Katie's parents, who were deeply religious,
were dead set against her playing blues and R and B
music. She was only officially allowed to play gospel and

classical piano. Her parents even went so far as to lock up the piano to try to keep her from playing unsupervised. But she was listening to Little Richard and Fats Domino, R and B and blues on the radio, and restrictions didn't stand a chance. (1)

In 1958, she cut her first single, "Baby, Baby," on the Kry label. She began playing sessions for producer J.D. Miller and cut a number of 45's for his Action, Rocko, and Spot labels. Overall, she recorded over 500 singles in the 50's and 60's. While she was performing with her own band, the Uptighters, in 1964, she performed a gig with Otis Redding that led to three years as his opening act, until his death in a plane crash in 1967.

In the 1970's, devastated by Redding's death and needing to care for her ailing parents, Katie put her career on hold, but when the opportunity came to tour in Europe in 1982, she grabbed it and her career was back on track. European audiences couldn't get enough, and she returned over 30 times. American audiences rediscovered her as she began to play major festivals.

"She can floor the timid listener," reported the Boston Globe. "Webster can say more about the pain of betrayal with one low, sad growl, and more about the joy of fighting back against cruel life with one teasing roll of her eyes, than most could write in a book."

In 1988, Webster joined many other fine blues artists on the Alligator record label, and when she cut her debut Alligator album, *Swamp Boogie Queen*, she got support on the record from Bonnie Raitt, Robert Cray, and Kim Wilson. She followed up with two more great recordings, *Two-Fisted Mama*, and *No Foolin'*, before disaster struck. In 1993, she suffered a stroke and lost the use of her left hand and most of her eyesight. But her voice remained strong, and she continued to make limited appearances until shortly before she died on September 5, 1999. She was 63 years old. (2)

For fans of Louisiana blues, her music, and her memory,
live on.

18. **FRANCINE REED**

Francine Reed was born in 1947 in Pembroke Township, Illinois. On her official website, Francine explains: 'I always say I was born singing. When the doctor slapped me on the ass, I went (singing) 'Look at me!'" (1)

Francine sang with her family from the time she was five. However, in one of the common themes of this book, she married early and the marriage didn't last, leaving her the single mother of four children. Therefore, she was not able to devote herself to her career until her children were grown. However, she always sang in local clubs around Chicago while working various day jobs to support her family.

Finally, in 1985, in Phoenix, Arizona, Francine was introduced to Lyle Lovett, who was looking for a vocalist for his band. Ms. Reed was a perfect choice, and she spent the next eight years touring with Lovett and his Large Band. She also contributed vocals to albums by Willie Nelson, Roy Orbison, and Delbert McClinton.

In the 1990's, Francine moved to Atlanta, and in 1995, she released her own first album, *I Want You to Love Me*, which went to number seven on the Billboard Blues charts. (2) Lyle returned the favor on this album by singing a duet with his longtime vocalist.

More than any one album, though, Francine is known for one song, which is a concert favorite, has appeared on two of her albums, and on Lyle Lovett's Live in Texas album from 1999. That song brings us back full circle to the roots of the blues: Ida Cox's "Wild Women Don't Get the Blues." When Francine sings:

"You never get nothing by being an angel child
You better change your ways and get real wild…"(3)

The audience buys it just like they bought it when Ida Cox sang it in the 1920's. The blues are timeless, and universal, especially when a woman is selling the song.

Francine Reed is wildly popular in Georgia. In 2003, Atlanta magazine stated that she was, at that time, "probably the most beloved singer in the city." (4) And for a lot of fans, that is still true today.

19. SAFFIRE

The only female blues group in this collection, Saffire is a sassy and thoroughly modern trio of unlikely vocal companions. Referring to themselves as "the Uppity Blues Women," they surely live up to the title. With songs like "Middle Age Boogie Blues," and "Ain't Gonna Hush," they lay it all on the line.

Saffire is made up of founding members Ann Rabson and Gaye Adegbalola and longtime member, Andra Faye McIntosh, who replaced Earline Lewis when she left the group.

Gaye Adegbalola was born in 1944 in Fedricksburg, Virginia, where she still lives with long time partner Suzanne Moe. Before becoming a full-time musician, she was honored as Virginia's Teacher of the Year in 1982. She has been an activist for civil rights, women's rights, and lesbian rights. She is a black woman and has been a single mother. All of this informs her singing, although it does not explain the sassiness and good humor of so much of Saffire's material. Or does it?

Ann Rabson was born in 1945 in New York City. She discovered the blues at age 4, listening to Big Bill Broonzy on the radio. She began as a guitar player, but at age 35, she decided to teach herself piano. She plays blues, boogie-woogie and classic barrelhouse style and is a member of the Boogie Woogie Hall of Fame. She is deeply involved in educational activities and blues workshops. Like Gaye, she records as a solo artist as well as with Saffire.

When bassist Earlene Lewis left the group, mandolin player Andra Faye was called to sit in on a session. She was very nervous, but in 1992 she joined the group as a full-time member. A former registered nurse, she quickly learned to be a proficient bassist as well as playing guitar, mandolin, and violin.

The members of Saffire have never played down their age. They sing about being middle-aged, lusty, opinionated, and strong. They tackle all the traditional blues subjects: sex, booze, misbehaving, and make it all a whole lot of fun. This is not to say that they can't handle heartbreak as well, as in the wrenching, "Blues for Sharon Bottoms." But it's the raunchy, lively fun of songs like "Bitch with a Bad Attitude," or "Silver Beaver," that sets these ladies aside and plants them solidly in the present and in the past,

entertaining the shades of Bessie Smith, Ida Cox, and

Sippie Wallace.

As Saffire sings,

"Age ain't nothin' but a number,

And like a fine wine,

You don't get older / you just get better"

and listening to them, you know that's the truth.

20. KOKO TAYLOR

Koko Taylor once said that blues was her life. "It's a true feeling that comes from the heart, not just something that comes out of my mouth," she said. (1) Taylor lived the blues right up until her death in 2009.

Taylor was born Cora Walton in Tennessee. In the 1950's she married a truck driver named Robert Taylor and moved from Memphis to Chicago, where she began singing the blues in clubs. Willie Dixion saw her in 1962, and his influence got her more exposure and the attention of Chess Records. At Chess, she recorded, "Wang Dang Doodle," a song previously recorded by Howlin' Wolf and which established Taylor's raucous, raw style. It was a hit, reaching number 4 on the R 'n B charts in 1966, and the biggest commercial success Taylor every had.

Despite the lack of hit singles, Koko Taylor was an enormous hit as a touring and recording act, gathering thousands of fans through her performances and becoming even more popular after signing with Alligator Records in 1975. She made 9 records with Alligator, and 8 of them were Grammy nominated. She won 25 W.C. Handy Music Awards (now renamed the Blues Music Awards), more than any other artist. She was inducted into the Blues Hall of Fame in 1997, and received a Blues Foundation Lifetime Achievement Award in 1999. Her work influenced just about every modern female blues artist, including Janis Joplin and Bonnie Raitt.

Prior to her death on June 3, 2009 at age 81, Taylor was still playing about 70 concerts a year. Her final concert was at The Blues Awards on May 7, 2009. The Blues Awards have since created an award for female blues singers, The Koko Taylor Award, in her honor.

Epilogue

So, what do we learn from these women? Women who sing the blues are unconventional, strong, opinionated, and willing to bare their hearts and souls. They embody and express the feelings, desires, joys, and sorrow of every woman, and in doing so, they have empowered and continue to empower us.

Whether they sang nearly 100 years ago or whether they are still singing now, they lift us up, they fill our hearts, and they give us strength through their singing, their tears, and their laughter. It's been said that "Well-behaved women seldom make history." Well, these women weren't well-behaved by society's standards, but they did, and still do, make history.

Bring on the next generation!

NOTES

Preface:

(1) Harrison, Daphne Duval. Black Pearls, Blues Queens of the 1920s. Brunswick: Rutgers University Press, 1990

1. Mamie Smith

(1)   Red Hot Jazz, "Mamie Smith," http://www.redhotjazz.com/

(2)   Kernfeld, Barry Dean (2002). "Mamie Smith", The New Grove Dictionary of Jazz, 2nd edition, vol. 3, London: MacMillan

(3)   Ibid.

(4)   The African American Registry, http://www.aaregistry.com/

2. Ma Rainey

(1) Mother of the Blues: A Study of Ma Rainey. Univ. of Massachusetts Press, 1981

(2)   Oakley, Giles. The Devil's Music, A History of the Blues. New York: Harvest/HBJ book, 1976

(3)   Quote from Ma Rainey Page: Lamda.net (1997.)

(4)   Ibid.

(5)   Blues.org/Hall of Fame 1983 Inductees

(6)   Rock and Roll Hall of Fame: Ma Rainey: rockhall.com

3. Bessie Smith

(1)   Albertson, Chris. Bessie. Stein and Day, (New York), 1972.

(2)   Brooks, E., The Bessie Smith Companion: A Critical and Detailed Appreciation of the Recordings, Da Capo Press (New York), 1982.

(3)   Donovon, Richard X. Black Musicians of America. National Book Company, 1991.

(4)   Calliope Film Resources. "The Classic Blues and the Women Who Sang Them." Copyright 2000 CFR. http://www.calliope.org/blues/blues2.html

(5)   Jarvis, Gail. "Remembering Bessie Smith,"
LewRockwell.com, 2001.

(6)   Ibid.

(7)   Quoted in "Interview with Christ Albertson," Jerry
Jazz Man, jerryjazzmusician.com.

(8)   See Albertson, Bessie.

(9)   See "Interview," jerryjazzmausician.com

(10)   Whitney, Russ."Reflections of 1920's and 1930's
Street Life in the Music of Bessie Smith,"
bluesnet.hub.org/, 1995.

(10)Bessie Smith, "Please Help Me Get Him Off My Mind",
New York: Empress Music, Inc., 1928.

   (11) Porter Grainger and Everett   Robins, 'Taint
Nobody's Biz-Ness If I Do, New York: MCA Music, 1922.

   (12) Albertson. Bessie.

   (13) See "Interview," above.

4. Ida Cox

(1) The African American Registry," Ida Cox, Blues
Woman of the Times,"

http://www.aaregistry.com/african_american_history/1379/I

da_Cox_Blues_woman_of_the_times

(2) Red Hot Jazz,"Ida Cox,"

http://www.redhotjazz.com/idacox.html

(3) Ida Cox, "Wild Women Don't Get the Blues," lyrics

from Lyrics.time, http://www.redhotjazz.com/idacox.html

 (4) Oliver, Paul. Ida Cox. in Kernfeld, Barry. ed. The New

Grove Dictionary of Jazz, 2nd Edition, Vol. 1. London:

MacMillan, 2002.

(5) Ibid., Red Hot Jazz.

5. Sister Rosetta Thorpe

 (1) Encyclopedia of Arkansas, "Sister Rosetta Tharpe,"

http://www.encyclopediaofarkansas.net/encyclopedia/entry

-detail.aspx?entryID=1781

(2) Livin' Blues, "Sister Rosetta Tharpe,"

http://www.livinblues.com/bluesrooms/sisterrosettatharpe.a

sp

6. Victoria Spivey

(1)   Red Hot Jazz, "Victoria Spivey,"

http://www.redhotjazz.com

(2)   Cohn, Lawrence, Nothing But the Blues: The Music

and the Musicians, 1993 Abbeville Publishing Group, New

YorkIbid.

(3)   Lyrics courtesy of Lyrics Download,

http://www.lyricsdownload.com

(4)   Cohn, Lawrence, Nothing But the Blues

(5)   Ibid.

7. Alberta Hunter

(1)   Calliope Film Resources. "The Classic Blues and

the Women Who Sang Them." Copyright 2000 CFR.

http://www.calliope.org/blues/blues2.html

(2)   Red Hot Jazz, Alberta Hunter:

http://www.redhotjazz.com/

(3)   Ibid.

(4)   Quoted in "The Bluesmen and Women: Alberta

Hunter," http://afgen.com/bluesmen.html

(5)   "Alberta Hunter," VH1.com,

http://www.vh1.com/artists/az/hunter_alberta/bio.jhtml

(6)   Quote from Thinkexist.com, http://thinkexist.com/

8. Memphis Minnie

(1)   Trail of the HellHound: Memphis Minnie- Memphis

School: National Park Service, http://www.nps.gov/

(2)   Del Rey, "Memphis Minnie: Guitar Queen,"

Acoustic Guitar Magazine, 1997, et al.

(3)   "Memphis Minnie," Wikipedia,

http://www.wikipedia.com

(4)   Del Rey, ibid.

(5)   Wikipedia, as above.

(6)   Broonzy, Bill, Big Bill's Blues: Cassell and Co,

London, 1956

(7)   Garon, Paul and Beth. Woman With Guitar: Memphis

Minnie's Blues. New York, NY: Da Capo Publishing, 1992.

9. Sippie Wallace

(1)   Red Hot Jazz: "Sippie Wallace,"

http://www.redhotjazz.com/

(2)   Lyrics obtained from Lyrics for All,

http://www.lyricsforall.com

(3)   "Wallace, Beulah Thomas," Handbook of Texas

Online,

http://www.tsha.utexas.edu/handbook/online/articles/WW/f

waal.html

(4)   "Woman Be Wise," The Bonnie Raitt Collection

(5)   "Texas History Highlights: Women in Music," Jay

Brakefield, Texas Almanac Online,

http://www.texasalmanac.com

10. Big Mama Thornton

(1)   Cohn, Lawrence, Nothing But the Blues: The Music

and the Musicians, 1993 Abbeville Publishing Group, New

York

(2)   Wikipedia: Big Mama Thornton,

http://www.wikipedia.com

(3)   "Willie Mae'Big Mama' Thornton,"

Thatsalabama.com

(4)   Sawyer, Charles, "Willie Mae'Big Mama' Thornton

1978"

http://www.people.fas.harvard.edu/~sawyer/thornton.html

(5)   Janis Joplin version, Ball and Chain, quoted on

Lyrics Freak, http://www.lyricsfreak.com

(6)   "Big Mama Thornton, the Blues and More!", African

American registry

11. Ruth Brown

(1)   "Ruth Brown," VH1 Artist Profile:

http://www.vh1.com

(2)   "How Ruth Got Her Groove Back," Kimberly Ridley,

Hope Magazine: March/April, 1998

(3)   Quoted in "How the Blues Affected Race Relations

in the United States," Grant, Jessica,

http://www.jessicagrant.net/thesis/dancing.html

(4)   VH1, et al.

(5)   Ridley, Hope Magagzine.

(6)   "Ruth Brown, R&B Singer and Actress, Dies at 78,"

New York Times, November 17, 2006

(7)   Ridley, Hope Magazine.

12. Janis Joplin

1. "The Offical Janis Joplin Site,"

http://www.officialjanis.com/

2. "Janis Joplin.net," http://www.janisjoplin.net/

3. "Janis Joplin," Rock and Roll Hall of Fame,

http://www.rockhall.com/inductee/janis-joplin

4. "Janis Joplin," Rolling Stone,

http://www.rollingstone.com/artists/janisjoplin

13. Etta James

(1) "Etta James," Rolling Stone,

http://www.rollingstone.com/artists/ettajames/biography

(2) Etta James, "I'd Rather Go Blind," lyrics courtesy of

lyricsmania,

http://www.rollingstone.com/artists/ettajames/biography

(3)Joy Bennett Kinnon, "At last! Etta James loses 200

pounds and finds a new zest for life," Ebony Magazine,

2003

(4) "Etta James Quotes," Brainyquotes.com,

http://www.brainyquote.com/

(5) Ibid.

14. Bonnie Raitt

(1) "Bonnie Raitt," Wikipedia,

http://en.wikipedia.org/wiki/Bonnie_Raitt

(2) "Bonnie Raitt Inductee Profile," Rock and Roll Hall of

Fame, http://en.wikipedia.org/wiki/Bonnie_Raitt

(3) Official Bonnie Raitt Website,

http://www.bonnieraitt.com

15. Irma Thomas

(1)   Jyrki Ilva, "Irma Thomas-The Soul Queen of New

Orleans, http://www.helsinki.fi/~ilva/irma.html

(2) Jeff Hannusch a.k.a. Almost Slim, I Hear You Knockin'. The Sound of New Orleans Rhythm & Blues. (1985)

(3) Ibid., Jyrki Ilva

16. Marcia Ball

(1)   "Marcia Ball," Rosebud Agency, http://www.rosebudus.com/ball/PresumedInnocent.html

(2)   Michael Parrish, "Marcia Ball," Dirty Linen, http://www.dirtynelson.com/linen/feature/62ball.html

(3)   The Official Marcia Ball Website, http://www.marciaball.com/

17. Katie Webster

(1) "Katie Webster," All Music Guide, http://wm01.allmusic.com/cg/amg.dll?p=amg&sql=11:lxoibk r96akn~T

(2) "Katie Webster," Alligator Records website, http://www.alligator.com/index.cfm?section=artists&artistID =20

18. Francine Reed

(1)   Official Francine Reed Website

(2)   "Francine Reed, Inducted 1997," Arizona Blues Hall of Fame, http://members.cox.net/jjp62/index1.html#table

(3)   Ida Cox, "Wild Women Don't Get the Blues," lyrics from Lyrics.time, http://www.redhotjazz.com/idacox.html

(4)   Atlanta Magazine, special music issue, June 2003.

19. Saffire

(1)   "Saffire -the Uppity Blues Women," MSN Music, http://music.msn.com/artist/?artist=16070565

(2)   Saffire-the Uppity Blues Women official website, http://www.uppityblueswomen.com/

20. Koko Taylor

(1)   The Official Koko Taylor Website,

http://www.kokotaylor.com/

(2)   Daily Telegraph, "Koko Taylor Obituary,"

http://www.telegraph.co.uk/news/obituaries/culture-

obituaries/music-obituaries/5446469/Koko-Taylor.html

(3)   Wikipedia, "Koko Taylor,"

http://en.wikipedia.org/wiki/Koko_Taylor

Bibliography

arrison, Daphne Duval. *Black Pearls, Blues Queens of the 1920s.* Brunswick: Rutgers University Press, 1990

Lieb, Sandra R. *Mother of the Blues: A Study of Ma Rainey.* Univ. of Massachusetts Press 1983

Oakley, Giles. *The Devil's Music, A History of the Blues.* New York: Harvest/HBJ book, 1976

Albertson, Chris. *Bessie.* Stein and Day, (New York), 1972.

Brooks, E., *The Bessie Smith Companion: A Critical and Detailed Appreciation of the Recordings*, Da Capo Press (New York), 1982.

Donovon, Richard X. *Black Musicians of America.* National Book Company, 1991.

Oliver, Paul. Ida Cox. in Kernfeld, Barry. ed. *The New Grove Dictionar yof Jazz, 2nd Edition, Vol. 1*. London: MacMillan, 2002

Cohn, Lawrence, *Nothing But the Blues: The Music and the Musicians*, Abbeville Publishing Group, New York: 1993

Broonzy, Bill. *Big Bill's Blues*, Cassell and Co, London, 1956

Garon, Paul and Beth. *Woman With Guitar: Memphis Minnie's Blues*. New York, NY: Da Capo Publishing, 1992.

Jeff Hannusch a.k.a. Almost Slim: *I Hear You Knockin'. The Sound of New Orleans* Rhythm & Blues. (1985)

AN INCOMPLETE DISCOGRAPHY

MAMIE SMITH

Complete Recorded Works, Vol. 1

Complete recorded Works, Vol. 2

Complete Recorded Works, Vol. 3

Complete Recorded Works, Vol. 4

Mamie Smith Vol. 1 (1920-1921)

Mamie Smith Vol. 2 (1921-1922

Mamie Smith Vol. 3 (1922-1923)

Mamie Smith Vol. 4 (1923-1942

The Essential

MA RAINEY

An Introduction To Ma Rainey

Black Cat Hoot Owl

Complete 1928 Sessions In Chronological Order

Complete Recorded Works Vol. 1

Complete Recorded Works Vol. 3 (1925-26)

Don't Fish In My Sea (2004)

Heroes Of The Blues: The Very Best Of Ma Rainey

Hustlin' Blues

Ma Rainey

Ma Rainey's Black Bottom

Paramounts: Chronologically, Vol. 2

Paramounts: Chronologically, Vol. 5

Presenting Ma Rainey

BESSIE SMITH

Complete Recordings Vol. 5

Itinerary Of A Genius

Empress Of The Blues: 1923-1933

Complete Recordings Vol. 1

Complete Recordings Vol. 2

Complete Recordings Vol. 4

Careless Love Remastered; Digipak

Undisputed Queen Of The Blues

Best Of Empress Of The

Complete Recordings Vol. 1

Complete Recordings Vol. 3

Complete Recordings Vol. 6

Complete Recordings Vol. 7

Complete Recordings Vol. 8

Empress Of The Blues

Essential Bessie Smith

Greatest Hits

Legendary Blues Recordings: Bessie Smith

Preachin The Blues

Quintessence - The Empress 1923-1933

Sweet Mistreater

IDA COX

Complete Recorded Works Vol. 2 (1924-25)

Complete Recorded Works Vol. 1 (1923) (1995)

Complete Recorded Works Vol. 3 (1925-27) (1995) Import

Complete Recorded Works Vol. 4 (1927-38) (1995) Import

Essential (2001)

Ida Cox V5 1939-1940 Import

Uncrowned Queen Of The Blues

SISTER ROSETTA THARPE

Gospels In Rhythm

The Best Gospel Of Sister Rosetta Tharpe

Sister Rosetta Tharpe

Gospel Train

Hot Club De France Concerts

Little Richard & Sister Rosetta Tharpe

Complete Sister Rosetta Tharpe Vol. 3: 1947-1951

Complete Sister Rosetta Tharpe Vol. 4: 1951-1953

VICTORIA SPIVEY

Complete Recorded Works, Vol. 1 (1926-1927)

Complete Recorded Works, Vol. 2 (1927-1929)

Complete Recorded Works, Vol. 2 (1927-1929)

Victoria Spivey & The Easy Riders Jazz Band CD (1990)

Blues Is Life

Essential Victoria Spivey, The

Complete Recorded Works, Vol. 3 (1929-1936)

Complete Recorded Works, Vol. 4 (1936-1937)

Woman Blues!

ALBERTA HUNTER

Glory of Alberta Hunter

Complete Recorded Works, Vol. 1 (1921-1923)

Downhearted Blues

Songs We Taught Your Mother (with Lucille Hegamin and

Victoria Spivey)

Complete Recorded Works, Vol. 3 (1924-27)

Complete Recorded Works, Vol. 4 (1927-46)

Complete Recorded Works, Vol. 2 (1923-24)

Young Alberta Hunter: The Twenties

Classic Alberta Hunter: The Thirties

My Castle's Rockin'

SIPPIE WALLACE

Complete Recorded Works Vol. 1 (1923-1925)

Complete Recorded Works Vol. 2 (1925-1945)

Women Be Wise (Import, Denmark)

Sippie Wallace Vol. 1 (1923-1925)

Sippie Wallace Vol. 2 (1925-1945)

When You're Hot You're Country

Mighty Tight Woman

Sippie

BIG MAMA THORNTON

Ball N' Chain

Vanguard Visionaries: Big Mama Thornton

With The Muddy Waters Blues Band: 1966

Hound Dog: The Peacock Recordings

1950-1953

Complete Vanguard Recordings

In Europe (1965)

Jail

Sassy Mama

RUTH BROWN

Ruth Brown

Miss Rhythm

The Best Thing That Ever Happened

1951-1953

The Essentials

Who Am I

1949-1950

Here's That Rainy Day

A Good Day For The Blues

Mama He Treats Your Daughter Mean & Other Favorites

R+B = Ruth Brown

Rockin' In Rhythm: The Best Of Ruth Brown

Live in London

The Songs Of My Life

Reflections of Love

Fine And Mellow

Walkin' in the Sun

Miss Rhythm: Greatest Hits & More

Blues On Broadway

Have A Good Time

Softly

Fine Brown Frame

Help a Good Girl Go Bad

Ruth Brown/Miss Rhythm

JANIS JOPLIN

18 Essential Songs

Greatest Hits

Big Brother & The Holding Company / Janis Joplin

Live At Winterland '68

Box Of Pearls: The Janis Joplin Collection

Collection

In Concert

I Got Dem Ol' Kozmic Blues Again Mama!

Pearl: Legacy Edition (1971) Remastered; Special Edition;

Digipak

Pearl (1971)

Essential Janis Joplin (2003) Limited Edition; Remastered

Collection

Farewell Song

Janis (1993) Box Set   Collector's Edition $17.58

Love, Janis

One Night With Janis

Super Hits

ETTA JAMES

At Last! (1961) Remastered

Blues To The Bone

12 Songs Of Christmas

Very Best Of Etta James Import; Boxed Set

All The Way

Love Songs

Definitive Collection

Love Songs

Best Of Etta James

Rocks The House

Her Best

Essential Etta James

20th Century Masters: The Millennium Collection: The Best

Of Etta James

Late Show

Mystery Lady: Songs Of Billie Holiday

Matriarch Of The Blues

Stickin' To My Guns

Come A Little Closer

Heart Of A Woman

Let's Roll

18 Greatest

20TH Century Masters: The Millennium Collection (2007)

Remastered

Best Of Etta James

BONNIE RAITT

Bonnie Raitt (1971) Remastered

Give It Up (1972) Remastered

Best Of Bonnie Raitt (2003) Remastered

Souls Alike

Home Plate (1975) Remastered

Luck Of The Draw

Takin' My Time (1973) Remastered

Longing In Their Hearts

Silver Lining

Glow (1979) Remastered

Streetlights (1974) Remastered

Road Tested

Bonnie Raitt And Friends

Bonnie Raitt Collection

Fundamental (1998)

Green Light (1982) Remastered

Nick Of Time (1989)

Nine Lives (1986) Remastered

Sweet Forgiveness (1977) Remastered

Road Tested

IRMA THOMAS

Ruler Of My Heart

Irma Thomas' Somebody Told Me

Irma Thomas Selected Hits

After the Rain

Soul Masters

If You Want It, Come And Get It

My Heart's In Memphis: The Songs Of Dan Penn

The Story Of My Life

Sweet Soul Queen of New Orleans: The Irma Thomas Collection

Time Is on My Side

Walk Around Heaven: New Orleans Soul Gospel

True Believer

Time Is On My Side: Best Of Irma Thomas Volume 1

Live! Simply The Best

Something Good: The Muscle Shoals Chess Sessions

The Way I Feel

The New Rules

Soul Queen Of New Orleans

Turn My World Around

MARCIA BALL

Dreams Come True (with LouAnn Barton and Angela

Strahli)

Let Me Play With Your Poodle

Live! Down The Road

Presumed Innocent

Blue House

Soulful Dress

Choices & Changes

Gatorhythms

Hot Tamale Baby

Sing It! (with Marcia Ball and Tracey Nelson)

So Many Rivers

KATIE WEBSTER

Deluxe Edition

No Foolin'

Two-Fisted Mama!

The Swamp Boogie Queen

I Know That's Right

FRANCINE REED

Blues Collection

American Roots: Blues

SAFFIRE

Renaissance

Deluxe Edition

Ain't Gonna Hush

Live and Uppity

The The Middle Aged Blues

Cleaning House

Old, New, Borrowed & Blue

Broadcasting

Hot Flash

The Uppity Blues Women

KOKO TAYLOR

Old School

Deluxe Edition

Royal Blue

Force of Nature\

Jump For Joy-AL4784

Live From Chicago--An Audience With The Queen

Queen of the Blue

From the Heart of a Woman-AL4724

EarthShaker

I Got What It Takes-AL4706

Koko Taylor

Basic Soul

South Side Baby (originally Black & Blue)

Made in the USA
Thornton, CO
10/13/23 16:29:31